BATTLEFIELD SUPPORT

GEOFF CORNISH

Lerner Publications Company
Minneapolis

First American edition published by Lerner Publications Company

Copyright © 2003 by The Brown Reference Group plc.

Lerner Publications Company.
A division of Lerner Publishing Group
241 First Avenue North
Minneapolis, MN55401 U.S.A.

Website address: www.lernerbooks.com

Library of Congress Cataloging-in-Publication Data

Cornish, Geoff.
 Battlefield support / by Geoff Cornish.
      p. cm. -- (Military hardware in action)
Includes index.
Summary: Profiles some of the different equipment and personnel that provide support services on the battlefield for the United States and other nations around the world.
  ISBN 0–8225–4708–2 (lib. bdg.)
1. Vehicles, Military—United States—Juvenile literature. 2. Logistics—Juvenile literature. 3. Airplanes, Military—United States—Juvenile literature. [1. Vehicles, Military. 2. Airplanes, Military.] I. Title. II. Series.
  UC343 .C67   2003
  623.7'4--dc21   2002152933

Printed in China
Bound in the United States of America
1 2 3 4 5 6 – OS – 08 07 06 05 04 03

This book uses black and yellow chevrons as a decorative element on some headers. They do not point to other elements on the page.

Contents

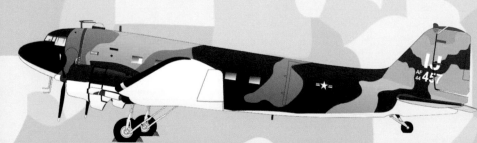

Introduction

A U.S. Air Force C5 Galaxy slowly drops from low clouds toward a small airstrip in the desert. After making a short landing roll, the plane opens its huge front cargo doors. Inside, a line of **armored fighting vehicles** (AFVs) waits to rumble down the ramp and into action. The C5 has just made a battle-zone delivery.

DOWN TO EARTH

A U.S. Air Force C5 Galaxy unloads an armored supply vehicle.

>> **armored fighting vehicle** = a battlefield vehicle with armor and weapons

Land, Sea, and Air

For every combat soldier, sailor, or pilot, a small army of support equipment and personnel provides essential back-up services. Ships, trucks, and airplanes carry supplies. Maintenance teams ensure that hardware is in working order. Medical personnel and equipment care for those wounded in combat.

GROUND SUPPORT

U.S. Marine engineers supervise as an M88 **armored recovery vehicle** rolls over a temporary bridge. These marines specialize in infantry support skills and equipment. Armored recovery vehicles collect damaged AFVs under fire, so they can be repaired and returned to service.

SUPPLIES AT SEA

A supply ship, called a tender (*center*), escorted by a cruiser (*right*), draws alongside a U.S. Navy aircraft carrier. Tenders bring fuel, food, and ammunition to warships at sea. They allow the warships to remain on duty for long periods. The process of transferring supplies from tender to ship is called replenishment at sea (RAS) or replenishment underway.

Air and Space

Battlefield support is just as important in the air as it is on the ground or at sea. Cargo airplanes deliver supplies to ground forces. Airplanes also carry out airborne refueling tasks and **reconnaissance** missions. Casualty evacuation (casevac) brings the wounded from the battlefield. Above the atmosphere are space satellites that provide information and communications vital to warfare at long range.

AIRBORNE GAS STATION

A B2 Spirit Stealth bomber takes on fuel from a U.S. Air Force KC135 Boeing Stratotanker. Air-to-air refueling lets combat airplanes fly longer missions. They can strike at enemy targets located at great distances from their base.

COMMAND AND CONTROL

This Boeing E3 Sentry carries an airborne warning and control system (**AWACS**). AWACS provides a high-level overview of the battle area. The sophisticated radar enables the aircraft to monitor what is happening on the ground, at sea, or in the air. AWACS crews can coordinate different battle forces to work together.

EYES IN SPACE

A military observation satellite is launched from Cape Canaveral in Florida. Space satellites carry high-tech equipment that can monitor what is happening, even through thick clouds or at night. Satellites are beyond the reach of conventional anti-aircraft missiles or guns.

CASEVAC

A U.S. Air Force flight surgeon looks after a wounded soldier on board a C141 Starlifter casualty evacuation airplane. Casevac is an important part of battlefield support. The faster the wounded can be brought to a field hospital, the greater are their chances of recovery.

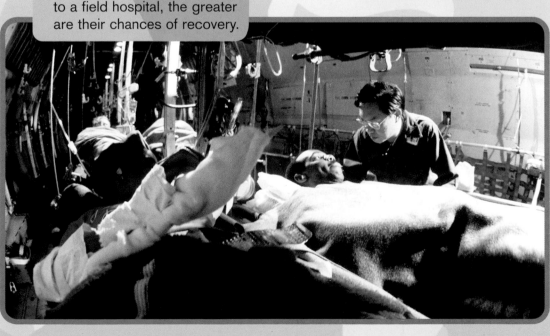

History

For as long as people have made war, frontline **combatants** have needed the support of others to bring fresh troops and materials to help them. For many centuries, armies relied on humans or pack animals to supply their needs. Ships have carried armies across the oceans since early times.

STEAM AGE

U.S. military railroad engine *W.H. Whiton* during the Civil War (1861–1865). In the mid-1800s, the steam engine and railroads changed the way materials and troops could be delivered to the battlefield.

WAGON TRAIN

Wagons gather at Brandy Station, Virginia, during the Civil War. Horse-drawn wagon trains or **baggage trains** were the normal means of transport for centuries.

TROOP SHIP

New York volunteers board a U.S. Army troop transport ship bound for Cuba during the Spanish American War (1898). To reach a battlefield overseas, armies relied on steamships to transport troops, horses, food, and weapons. Rough seas and tight spaces made these journeys very uncomfortable. Enemy attack was an additional danger.

Global Warfare

Mechanization and industrialization changed the way wars were fought at the start of the 1900s. **Communication lines** became longer, so wars could be fought at greater distances from home base.

World War I

World War I (1914–1918) may have been fought according to the railroad timetables of Europe. Military commanders had to take into account the time taken for troop trains to reach the front when planning major attacks.

BATTLE BUSES

A line of Paris city buses carries French troops to the front in 1914. British forces in France also used double-decker London buses as troop transports to ferry soldiers to the trenches.

AERIAL OBSERVATION

A balloon observer during World War I. Watching enemy movements is an important support role. By looking down from a hill or other high point, observers can see how the enemy is placed to attack. Balloons were used in both the Civil War and World War I for observing enemy positions. By World War I, reconnaissance airplanes had also become available. They could move faster, see more, and avoid enemy groundfire.

CONVOYS

The United States joined the war in 1917. Troops and equipment were shipped across the Atlantic to Europe in converted cargo ships. These supply ships were under constant threat from German submarines. Ships sailed in **convoys**, escorted by warships for protection.

Specialization

By World War II (1939–1945), ships, airplanes, and armored vehicles had been developed for the sole purpose of delivering supplies and services to the battle zone. In earlier times, horses could be fed from the countryside. In contrast, mechanized warfare required huge quantities of fuel and other support.

ALL-AROUNDER

A German Junkers Ju52 supply plane takes off during World War II. The Ju52 was a three-engine transport converted from a civilian airliner. It was used for carrying troops and equipment, for aerial observation, for parachute drops, and as a **glider tug**.

"GOONEY BIRD"

A U.S. Douglas C47, popularly known as the "Gooney Bird." The C47 was the most famous transport airplane of World War II. Like the German Ju52, it was converted from a civilian airliner, the 1935 DC3. It was used for all kinds of support missions. Many are still flying throughout the world.

>> **glider tug** = an aircraft that tows a glider into the air

SEABEES

This armored vehicle belongs to a construction battalion (known as a "Seabee"). The vehicle carries a large boulder needed to plug a seawall during World War II. Seabees are required to build and maintain **fortifications** and carry out all kinds of construction work in a battle zone.

FIRST AID

A Mobile Army Surgical Hospital (MASH) was set up at Wonju during the Korean War (1950–1953). Casualties were often brought in from the battlefield by helicopter. Many lives were saved because soldiers were treated soon after being wounded.

>> **fortification** = any artificial defensive structure

Supplying the Troops

The French general Napoleon Bonaparte once said that an army marches on its stomach. He meant that, to fight effectively, an army needs to be well provided with food, clothing, and ammunition. Supplying a modern army is still an important goal. However, the distances are often greater, and speed is even more essential.

AIRBORNE

Troops of the U.S. 82nd Airborne Division line up to board a U.S. Air Force C17 Globemaster on their way to a battle zone. These big lifters can carry more than 100 fully equipped troops across the world in hours. By comparison, the U.S. troops of World War I spent several weeks onboard ships crossing the Atlantic to reach the battlefields of Europe.

ACROSS THE WATER

A truck tows a 155mm M198 **howitzer** ashore from an air-cushion landing craft (ACLC) during operations in Somalia in 1993. Landing craft ferry equipment and personnel between the shore and supply ships moored far out to sea.

HUMVEE

A U.S. Marine Corps M998 Humvee is fitted with snow tracks for mountain and arctic warfare. The Humvee is a light armored vehicle that can survive small-arms fire, mines, and grenade attacks. Humvees are used for reconnaissance, for troop transport, and as **TOW** missile carriers. They are very tough and can be adapted for many different jobs and terrains.

World Wars

In World War I, most of the fighting took place in a small area of northern Europe. By World War II, however, warfare was truly worldwide. The period saw some of the most spectacular advances in the technology and organization of long-range supply operations.

LIBERTY SHIPS

A convoy of Liberty Ships carrying war supplies to Europe crosses the Atlantic during World War II. An industrialist, Henry J. Kaiser, organized the Liberty Ship program. He brought the latest **mass-production** techniques to the shipyards. By building parts at factories all over the United States, he was able to assemble ships at an incredibly fast rate. In all, U.S. workers built more than 2,000 Liberty Ships between 1941 and 1945. They had achieved a rate of one ship every day by 1945.

WOMEN WELDERS

Women shipworkers were photographed in Pascagoula, Mississippi, in 1943. Nearly all of the workers who built Liberty Ships had little or no previous experience of shipbuilding.

D Day

Allied forces launched their invasion of German-occupied Europe on June 6, 1944, known as D day. It was the beginning of the end of the war in Europe. But D day itself was the result of two years of planning and **logistical** preparations.

DECISIVE

General Dwight D. Eisenhower became supreme allied commander in 1943. He organized an invasion force of 5,000 tanks and guns, 6,000 airplanes, and 1,000 ships. More than 156,000 soldiers, sailors, and marines took part. The planning was effective, and the victory was decisive.

Battlefield Transport

Being able to move troops quickly and safely around a battle zone can make the difference between failure and success. Armored personnel carriers (APCs) are built for this purpose.

BATTLE BUS

A U.S. Army Bradley M3 Cavalry Fighting Vehicle cruises through the desert in Saudi Arabia in 1992. The Bradley can carry up to eleven fully equipped troops. It provides armored protection from bullets, grenades, and most mines.

ALL-AROUNDER

The jeep had a military career lasting from the early 1940s to the early 1970s. It was a lightweight, four-seat, all-terrain utility vehicle. The jeep earned its place in history as a tough and reliable all-arounder. Many jeeps are still in service with armed forces around the world. Many more have found enthusiastic civilian owners and restorers.

GENERAL PURPOSE

"Jeep" came from the name general purpose (GP) vehicle. About 360,000 Willys-Overland jeeps were produced during the World War II period.

>> **mobilized** = made ready for sending into combat

Enduring Freedom

After the September 11 attacks on the United States in 2001, U.S. forces were rapidly **mobilized** to take the war to the terrorists hiding in Afghanistan. Operation Enduring Freedom involved transporting thousands of combatants and their supplies from the United States to locations in southwestern Asia.

LOADING

U.S. Army personnel load cartons of supplies onto pallets for an **airlift** to Afghanistan.

>> **airlift** = the transport of cargo or personnel by aircraft

Engineers and Other Experts

Engineers, mechanics, electricians, explosives experts, and computer technicians all bring needed skills to an armed force in combat. They build, repair, and maintain all the equipment necessary to keep ahead of the enemy.

KEEP 'EM FLYING

Royal Air Force (RAF) maintenance crews work hard to repair a bomb-damaged British Hawker Typhoon fighter during World War II. Modern airplanes are more sophisticated than the Typhoon, but the crew's job is basically the same—get the plane back in the air.

KEEP 'EM ROLLING

U.S. Army personnel carry out engine maintenance on an M113 armored personnel carrier in the Sahara Desert. Desert sandstorms can sometimes do as much damage to the motors and mechanical parts of an armored vehicle as enemy action. Grit clogs the moving parts.

KEEP 'EM AFLOAT

U.S. Navy personnel attach a **refueling probe** from the military sealift command ship USS *Rappahannock* to the receiver nozzle aboard the amphibious command ship USS *Blue Ridge*. RAS allows ships to remain **on station** without having to return to base for fuel.

Construction

When we think of war, we think of destruction. But construction is also an important part of military preparation and planning in any combat zone. Seabees, the U.S. Navy's construction battalions, have the job of building defenses and other important structures.

BUILD AND FIGHT

A U.S. Navy Seabee at the controls of a bulldozer. "We build, we fight" is their motto. From the Pacific islands of World War II to the deserts of Afghanistan, men and women of the Seabees have built entire bases. They have bulldozed and paved thousands of miles of airstrips and roads and have put up countless buildings and bridges.

>> **deploying** = a military term meaning putting into place

GETTING ACROSS

An M60 bridge-laying tank does its job during operations in Bosnia in the 1990s. Rivers and canals can protect defenders from their attackers. By **deploying** instant bridges for AFVs and troops, an attacking force can rapidly overcome such natural barriers.

TENT CITY

U.S. Army construction teams built this temporary camp in Afghanistan. The camp housed troops airlifted from the United States as part of Operation Enduring Freedom in 2002. Aside from putting up hundreds of tents, the teams also provided fresh water and an electricity **generator**.

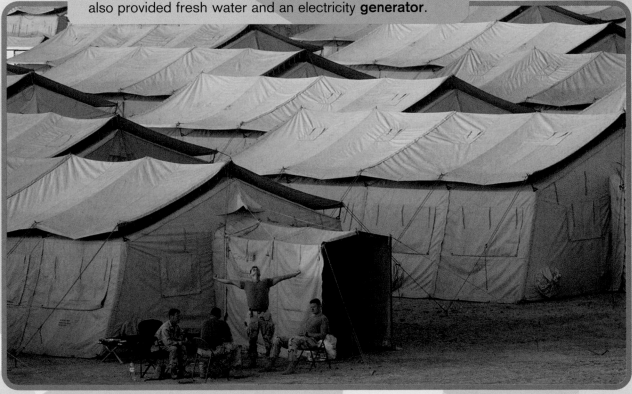

>> **generator** = a motor that creates an electrical power supply

Making the Way Safe

One of the most important and dangerous jobs in a combat area is clearing mines and **unexploded ordnance**. Many modern land mines are made almost entirely of plastic. They are difficult to find. Unexploded bombs and shells are especially hazardous. They can sometimes be set off just by touch or even by ground vibration.

WAY CLEAR

This Abrams M1A1 tank has a mine-clearing plow fitted on the front. The steel plow pushes away or sets off anti-tank mines before they can destroy the tank.

SEA THREAT

An Explosive Ordnance Disposal (EOD) officer inspects an Iraqi sea mine in the Persian Gulf during Operation Desert Storm. Mines like this damaged several U.S. ships, but navy **salvage** teams soon repaired them.

PATCH UP

Repair crews inspect damage caused by an Iraqi mine to the hull of the amphibious assault ship USS *Tripoli* in 1991. The ship was able to continue operating after temporary repairs were made.

SALVAGE

The marine salvage and rescue ship USS *Beaufort* awaits orders. Salvage and rescue ships are designed to help ships that have been damaged by mines or other weapons.

Reconnaissance

Reconnaissance means observing what the enemy is doing. Reconnaissance is a part of intelligence, which also includes finding out what the enemy is planning to do or has already done.

Prying Eyes

There are many different ways of watching an enemy. These include field observation, aerial photography, and radio interception. **Infiltration** and **satellite imaging** are also part of reconnaissance.

LOOKING DOWN

A U.S. Army observer shows how to use a ground reconnaissance camera from the open cockpit of a World War I airplane. Photography and aviation were new technologies in the early 1900s. Aerial photography was a state-of-the-art way to gather intelligence.

>> **infiltration** = undercover observation inside enemy territory

COLD WARFARE

A Lockheed U2 spyplane flies over mountainous territory. The U.S. Air Force carried out many high-level photographic reconnaissance missions over the Soviet Union in the 1950s. The U2 flew above the range of Soviet fighters and surface-to-air missiles.

SPACE AGE

A satellite image shows Iraq's capital city of Baghdad. Space satellites can observe more than airplanes and cannot be brought down by anti-aircraft weapons.

AIRWAVES

Radio technicians set up a field signals intelligence station during Operation Enduring Freedom in Afghanistan in 2002. Signals intelligence means listening in to enemy radio communications. Military radio signals are usually transmitted in code and at very high speeds. However, skilled personnel and sophisticated computers can often make them understood.

Early Warning

Being able to detect enemy missiles or aircraft before they can attack is vital for defense. Some ships, airplanes, and vehicles have been developed especially for this purpose.

AIR WATCH

An E2 Hawkeye early warning aircraft is catapulted from the deck of the USS *Saratoga* during Operation Desert Storm. The E2 is equipped with long-range airborne radar. This equipment finds approaching enemy aircraft or ships before they come within attacking range.

SEA WATCH

The amphibious command ship USS *Blue Ridge* uses its high-tech computer equipment to warn other ships of attack. The ship gathers all radio, satellite, and airplane intelligence. It is the ears and eyes of the **battle group** at sea.

GROUND WATCH

The Parakeet tactical satellite communications system can receive and transmit **satellite data** in a battle area. This gives local commanders an overview of what is happening around them. Parakeet has protective armor plating and is mobile. It keeps in step with the fighting forces.

Battle Support Enemies

Much battlefield support equipment is similar to combat equipment. Support ships, airplanes, and vehicles are all at risk from the same threats as other **military assets**. But, as noncombatant equipment, they usually do not have the same amount of defensive hardware.

EASY PICKINGS

A German U-boat (submarine) surfaces during World War II. U-boats were a constant menace to slow and unarmed supply ships traveling between North America and Europe during both world wars. Millions of tons of much-needed war material were lost from submarine attack. The supply ships countered this threat by sailing in convoys with warships to protect them.

AIR-TO-AIR

A U.S. Air Force F22 Raptor launches its Sidewinder air-to-air missile. Air-to-air missiles can threaten airplanes like the Boeing AWACs or E2 Hawkeye. Without these eyes in the sky, friendly surface forces are at greater risk from unseen attack.

>> **military asset** = hardware or personnel needed for combat

From the Ground Up

Missiles launched from the ground or from warships at sea are another hazard, especially to low-flying aircraft.

STRIKE FROM THE SKY

A Russian air force Sukhoi Su30 strike airplane fires its laser-guided missile at a ground target below. Accurate air strikes on **supply columns** can starve ground forces of vital ammunition and equipment.

Enemies

Artillery, armored fighting vehicles (such as tanks), mortars, mines, and surface-to-surface missiles all represent a danger to battlefield support equipment and personnel.

MINE

A soldier places a land mine along an unpaved road. Motorized supply columns often use roads. Wheeled vehicles can travel quickly by road. They do not have the problem of navigating over open terrain. But roads are easy to ambush. Rough roads can conceal buried land mines.

BY HAND

Spotters with field glasses help to locate a target for a soldier armed with a TOW anti-tank missile. A single infantry soldier armed with a hand-held wire-guided missile, such as TOW, can destroy a truck or even bring down an aircraft.

SHAKE 'EM OFF

A U.S. Air Force C17 Globemaster transport airplane fires defensive **flares**. Flares can confuse the guidance systems of heat-seeking missiles, sending them off course.

>> **flare** = a bright, illuminated projectile like a firework

Support Hardware

Many different kinds of equipment are used to support fighting forces in the battlefield. All types of vehicles, aircraft, and vessels have been developed or adapted to supply the needs of frontline combatants.

C5 GALAXY

The Lockheed C5 Galaxy is one of the largest airplanes in the world. The C5 can transport troops, helicopters, armored vehicles, artillery, and all kinds of provisions (food, clothing, etc.). With air-to-air refueling, it can remain airborne as long as it has crewmembers to operate it.

Details:
Crew: 7
Length: 247 ft. 10 in.
Wingspan: 222 ft. 9 in.
Propulsion: 4 x 41,000-lb thrust **turbofans**
Max Speed: 541 mph
Ceiling: 34,000 ft.
Load: 291,000 lbs.

SR71 BLACKBIRD

The SR71 Blackbird was developed at the famous Lockheed "Skunk Works" during the 1960s. It is still the world's fastest and highest-flying airplane. It cannot easily be seen by radar and was designed for high altitude reconnaissance missions.

Details:
Crew: 2
Length: 107 ft. 5 in.
Wingspan: 55 ft. 6 in.
Propulsion: 2 x 32,500-lb thrust turbojets
Max Speed: 2,200 mph
Ceiling: 85,000 ft.
Range: 2,000 mi.

KC10 EXTENDER

The U.S. Air Force KC10 Extender (shown refueling a B2 Spirit bomber) is an air-to-air refueling airplane developed from the commercial DC10 airliner. It can refuel fighters, bombers, and long-range cargo aircraft. The fuel is delivered via a boom that trails from the belly of the airplane.

Details:
Crew: 4
Length: 181 ft. 7 in.
Wingspan: 165 ft. 4 in.
Propulsion: 3 x 52,500-lb thrust turbofans
Max Speed: 619 mph
Ceiling: 42,000 ft.
Load: 342,000 lbs. fuel

Support Hardware

Support at sea includes extra oil-refueling ships and other supply ships, landing craft, and offshore salvage and repair ships. Intelligence-gathering ships and spy ships are also an important source of information during a conflict.

LCU MK10

The landing craft utility (LCU) is a long-range **beach assault craft** for ferrying troops and armored vehicles ashore. It has armored sides as protection against an opposed landing.

Details:
Crew: 13
Length: 174 ft.
Beam: 42 ft.
Propulsion: 4 x 250 hp diesels, 2 shafts
Max Speed: 15 kts.
Displacement: 575 tons
Load: 170 tons

USS *CALOOSAHATCHEE*

The USS *Caloosahatchee* was a fleet oiler with the U.S. Navy. It supplied fuel to warships at sea in the process known as replenishment underway. The U.S. Navy's Military Sealift Command increasingly uses civilian ships for this purpose.

Details:
Crew: 22 officers, 362 enlisted
Length: 644 ft.
Beam: 75 ft.
Propulsion: 1 x 13,500 hp steam turbine, 2 shafts
Max Speed: 18 kts.
Displacement: 34,750 tons
Load: 24,000 tons

>> **beach assault craft** = a ship that can land onshore to let off troops

USS DOLPHIN

The USS *Dolphin* is a U.S. Navy research and development submarine. It is used to test **sonar** systems, laser communications, and missile tracking and in deep-sea submarine operations. The *Dolphin* also carries equipment for surveillance of enemy communications and underwater warfare systems.

Details:
Crew: 5 officers, 46 enlisted
Length: 165 ft.
Beam: 18 ft.
Propulsion: 2 x 425 hp diesel electric motor
Max Speed: 10 kts.
Displacement: 950 tons
Load: 12 tons

>> **sonar** = an underwater listening and locating system

Support Hardware

Logistics and supply are not just about the vehicles used for transport themselves. Roads have to be built, rivers bridged, and mountains crossed for the vehicles to make their much-needed deliveries.

M60 ARMORED VEHICLE LAUNCHED BRIDGE

The M60 armored vehicle launched bridge (AVLB) is based on the **hull** of an M60 tank. In place of the guns is a folding bridge that can be laid across rivers or deep trenches. The bridge is strong enough to support an Abrams M1 tank.

Details:
Crew: 2
Length: 31 ft.
Weight: 56.6 tons
Road Speed: 12 mph
Range: 290 mi.
Bridge: 63 ft. extended
Propulsion: 12-cylinder diesel engine

>> **hull** = the main body of a tank, without the turret and main gun

M728

This U.S. Army M728 has a mine-clearing rake attached to the front. The M728 is also equipped with a **demolition gun**. The mine rake was specially designed for the sandy conditions of Operation Desert Storm in 1991.

Details:
Crew: 4
Length: 30 ft.
Weight: 50 tons
Road Speed: 24 mph
Range: 290 mi.
Armament: 165mm demolition gun,
　　2 x 7.62mm machine guns
Propulsion: 12-cylinder diesel engine

CH47 CHINOOK

The CH47 improved cargo helicopter is an updated version of the long-serving Chinook. It has proven to be a reliable heavy lifter over several decades. The design looks set to continue in service well into the 2000s.

Details:
Crew: 2
Length: 50 ft.
Width: 14 ft. 9 in.
Propulsion: 2 x 1770 hp turboshaft engines
Max Speed: 167 mph
Ceiling: 10,000 ft.
Load: 16,000 lbs.

Future Combat Support

Logistic and battlefield support hardware of the future will rely more on robotics and less on people. Unmanned aerial vehicles will take over more of the battlefield communications and reconnaissance missions carried out by aircraft with crews. Satellites and other space technologies will continue to improve long-range intelligence gathering.

LANCER

The Lancer is the medium armored fighting vehicle of the future. The Lancer will have completely computerized, unmanned guns that will respond to commands from **remote sensors**. Coded radio information and commands will be received through the equipment mounted on the gun turret.

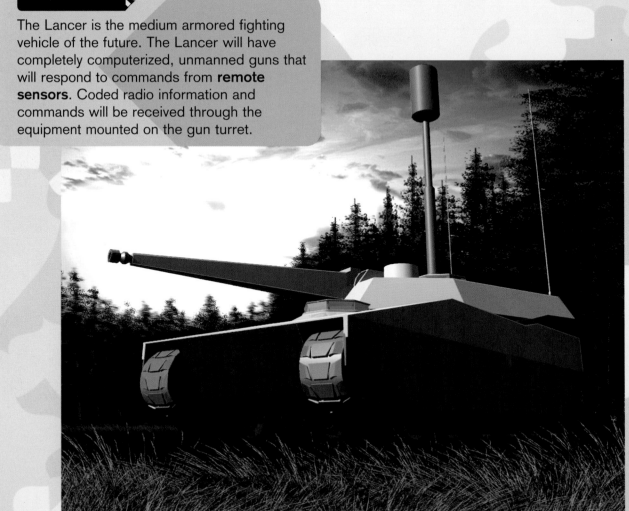

>> **remote sensor** = equipment that sends information by radio

Planes without Crews

PHOENIX

A Phoenix experimental unmanned aerial reconnaissance vehicle leaves its launcher. The Phoenix is one of many pilotless designs. A pilotless aircraft is cheaper, quieter, and lighter than a conventional airplane. No lives are at risk if it is brought down.

DIGITAL DETAIL

Computerized **image analysis** will replace old-style reconnaissance photography. The new satellite images use high-tech graphics to produce more detailed information about enemy movements.

Future Combat Support

Stealth technology and sophisticated communications systems are already important on the front line. These improvements will be just as key in battlefield support roles.

People and Machines

The key to successfully operating unmanned crafts will be the communications network that links them to their human controllers.

SENSOR-TO-SENSOR

This illustration shows how future battlefield equipment will link unmanned airborne strike vehicles to piloted control aircraft. Onboard computers will enable the manned airplanes *(foreground)* to direct the unmanned strike vehicles toward the intended target.

>> **stealth technology** = design making hardware difficult to detect

Satellites, computers, and reconnaissance equipment are already important on the front line. These improvements will be just as key in battlefield support roles. Future military authorities will be able to plan and follow missions from their computer screens far from the combat area. They will be able to direct field commanders while a battle is in progress, anywhere in the world.

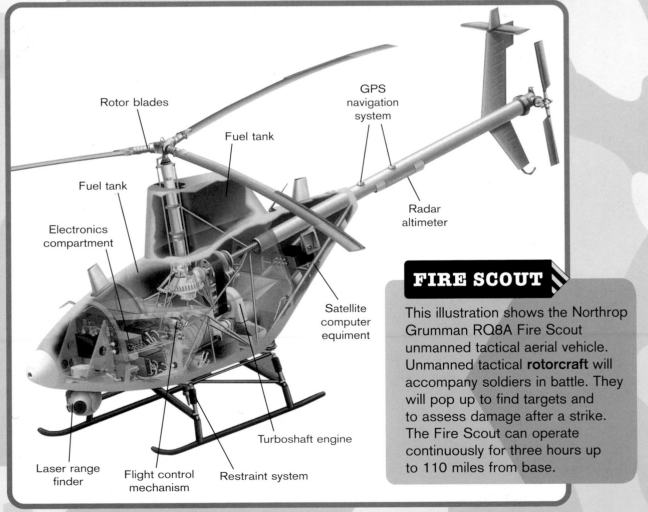

Rotor blades

GPS navigation system

Fuel tank

Fuel tank

Radar altimeter

Electronics compartment

Satellite computer equiment

FIRE SCOUT

This illustration shows the Northrop Grumman RQ8A Fire Scout unmanned tactical aerial vehicle. Unmanned tactical **rotorcraft** will accompany soldiers in battle. They will pop up to find targets and to assess damage after a strike. The Fire Scout can operate continuously for three hours up to 110 miles from base.

Turboshaft engine

Laser range finder

Flight control mechanism

Restraint system

Future Combat Support

High-tech electronics and unmanned equipment will be important in the future. But combat supply missions will still rely on trucks, ships, and airplanes to carry the materials and equipment needed for military actions.

STEALTHY SUPPORT

This computer image shows a future **strategic** transport aircraft. This design brings together stealth and high speed. The airplane will be as large as a C130 Hercules cargo plane. It will probably reach flying speeds faster than the speed of sound.

BAY CLASS

Britain's Royal Navy is planning a new Bay class of large amphibious assault ships. They will easily transport troops and armored vehicles directly into combat. This will allow them to discharge their personnel and equipment directly onto a beach without having to drop anchor.

CONSTANT IMPROVEMENT

Technicians install new **avionics** in a U.S. Air Force air-launch cruise missile. New developments keep the military supplied with weapons for the future. Manufacturers and maintenance crews work continuously on update programs. Their job is to equip hardware already proven in combat with new engines, electronics, and computer-control systems to help keep them effective.

>> **avionics** = electronic aircraft instruments and control systems

Hardware at a Glance

ACLC = air cushion landing craft
AFV = armored fighting vehicle
ALSL = alternative landing ship logistics
APC = armored personnel carrier
ASW = anti-submarine warfare
AVLB = armored vehicle launched bridge
AWACS = airborne warning and control
    system
EOD = explosives ordnance disposal

ICH = improved cargo helicopter
LCU = landing craft utility
MASH = Mobile Army Surgical Hospital
RAS = replenishment at sea
SEAL = Sea/Air/Land Special Forces
SIGINT = signals intelligence
TOW = tube-launched, optically-tracked, wire-
    guided
UTAV = unmanned tactical aerial vehicle

Further Reading & Websites

Ambrose, Stephen E. *The Good Fight: How World War II Was Won.* New York: Atheneum, 2001.

Bartlett, Richard. *Army Fighting Vehicles.* New York: Heinemann Library, 2003.

Bartlett, Richard. *United States Navy.* New York: Heinemann Library, 2003.

Baysura, Kelly. *Cargo Planes: Flying Machines.* Vero Beach, FL: Rourke Book Company, 2001.

Chant, Christopher. *The History of the World's Warships.* New York: Book Sales, 2000.

Faulkner, Keith. *Jane's Warship Recognition Guide.* New York: HarperResource, 1999.

Grant, George. *Warships: from the Galley to the Present Day.* New York: Gramercy, 2001.

Guetat, Gerald. *Liberty Ship.* Osceola, WI: Motorbooks International, 2002.

Holden, Henry M. *Rescue Helicopters and Aircraft.* Berkeley Heights, NJ: Enslow Publishing, 2002.

Kuhn, Betsy. *Angels of Mercy: The Army Nurses of World War II.* New York: Atheneum, 1999.

Loves, June. *Military Aircraft.* Broomall, PA: Chelsea House, 2001.

Miller, D. M. O. *The Illustrated Directory of Warships.* Osceola, WI: Motorbooks International, 2001.

Russell, Alan K. *Modern Battle Tanks and Support Vehicles.* Mechanicsburg PA: Stackpole Books,1997.

Center of Military History <http://www.army.mil/cmh-pg>
Naval Construction Force <http://www.seabee.navy.mil>
Royal Canadian Armoured Corps School <http://www.army.dnd.ca>
U.S. Marine Corps <http://www.usmc.mil>

Places to Visit

You can see examples of some of the combat support hardware contained in this book by visiting the military and maritime museums listed here.

Air Mobility Command Museum, Dover AFB, Delaware <http://amcmuseum.org>

Canadian War Museum. Ottawa, Ontario, Canada <www.civilization.ca/cwm/cwme.asp>

Great Lakes Naval Memorial & Museum, Muskegon, Michigan <www.silversides.org>

Hampton Roads Naval Museum, Norfolk, Virginia <www.hrnm.navy.mil>

Heartland Museum of Military Vehicles, Lexington, Nebraska <www.heartlandmuseum.com>

Intrepid Sea-Air-Space Museum, New York, New York <www.intrepidmusuem.org>

Louisiana Naval War Memorial, Baton Rouge, Louisiana <www.usskidd.com>

Marine Corps Air Ground Museum, Quantico, Virginia

Maritime Command Museum, Halifax, Nova Scotia, Canada
    <www.pspmembers.com/marcommuseum/>

Military Vehicle Museum, South El Monte, California
    <http://hometown.aol.com/tankland/museum/htm>

National D Day Museum, New Orleans, Louisiana <www.ddaymuseum.org/index.html?bhcp=1>

National Museum of Naval Aviation, Pensacola, Florida <www.naval-air.org>

San Diego Maritime Museum, San Diego, California <www.sdmaritime.com>

Springfield Armory Museum, Springfield, Massachusetts <www.nps.gov/spar/>

U.S. Air Force Museum, Wright-Patterson AFB, Dayton, Ohio <www.wpafb.af.mil/museum/>

U.S. Army Engineer Museum, Ft. Leonard Wood, Missouri
    <www.wood.army.mil/museum/default.htm>

U.S. Army Medical Department Museum, Ft. Sam Houston, Virginia
    <www.cs.amedd.army.mil/dptmsec/amedd.htm>

U.S. Army Transportation Museum, Ft. Eustis, Virginia
    <www.eustis.army.mil/dptmsec/museum.htm>

Vallejo Naval and Historical Museum, Vallejo, California <www.vallejomuseum.org>

Virginia War Museum, Newport News, Virginia <www.warmuseum.org>

Washington Navy Yard Museum, Washington, D.C.
    <www.history.navy.mil/branches/nhcorg8.htm>

Index

Picture Sources